MW01002066

# I've Just Started Living

by Priscilla McGruder
with
Judith Bentley

Insignia Publications
Sacramento, California

# I've Just Started Living
by Priscilla McGruder
  with Judith Bentley

Copyright 2004: Carroll & Priscilla McGruder

Library of Congress Control Number 2003116963
ISBN 0-9748100-0-2

> **Advisory**
>     Readers are advised to consult with their physician or other medical practitioner before implementing the suggestions that follow.
>     This book is not intended to take the place of sound medical advice or to treat specific maladies. Neither the author nor the publisher assumes any liability for the possible adverse consequences as a result of the information contained herein.

All Scripture quotations are from the King James Version of the Bible unless otherwise identified.

McGruder Ministries Inc.
P.O. Box 764
Kennett, MO 63857
Ph. 573-888-9096

Cover design by Paul Povolni
Text design by Debbie Patrick

Insignia Publications
Sacramento, California
(877) 413-1100

# I've Just Started Living

by Priscilla McGruder
with Judith Bentley

# Table of Contents

# Editorial Staff

Melanie Nordstrom

Kristin Hoover

Catherine Chambers

Orvada Churchill

With special thanks to
Carroll McGruder and Robert Bentley
for their many contributions
of time and talent.

# Meet Priscilla McGruder

*The singing McGruders have been a great force in the world of Gospel music. Priscilla has been a vital part of the group. Her husband, Carroll, has written many of the songs that have hit the top of the charts. Priscilla has often been the gifted soloist who has made the songs live in the hearts of people everywhere.*

*Priscilla is also the beloved pastor's wife of First United Pentecostal Church of Kennett, Missouri as well as the mother of three children--Eric, Shawnee, and Holly, and the grandmother of five.*

*She has committed her life to worshipping God, no matter where she may be. Her discovery and subsequent treatment of breast cancer put her faith to the supreme test. Now instead of worshipping God in beautiful churches or convention centers, she would find herself worshipping her Lord in doctor's offices and hospital corridors. Through the struggle, her faith came through as gold. May her spiritual journey inspire you as you read this unique story.*

# From the Pen
# of Judith Bentley

I touched the pages of the red spiral notebook with a sacred awe. It was Priscilla McGruder's journal of her journey with cancer. The first sentence that I scanned said, "Today I arose early and had sweet communion with the Lord." The sentence echoed throughout the book. I knew immediately that what I was touching was holy. It was God's words spoken directly to "Miss Priscilla", and now she was sharing them with me.

I knew that the next few weeks of consulting and writing and getting the story straight, would lead me into fresh spiritual waters. I was anxious to embark.

This book is more than just another cancer story. It is the story of a woman's direct communication with God. It is the words of a loving God who trusts a lady with some of His best secrets.

Today I faced a mountain
That I have no strength to climb
For the struggle of this journey's
left me weak
Both in body and in mind.
Where I stand to the peak
Is a distance on my own
I cannot reach
So the journey of a thousand
steps begins
Right here on my knees.

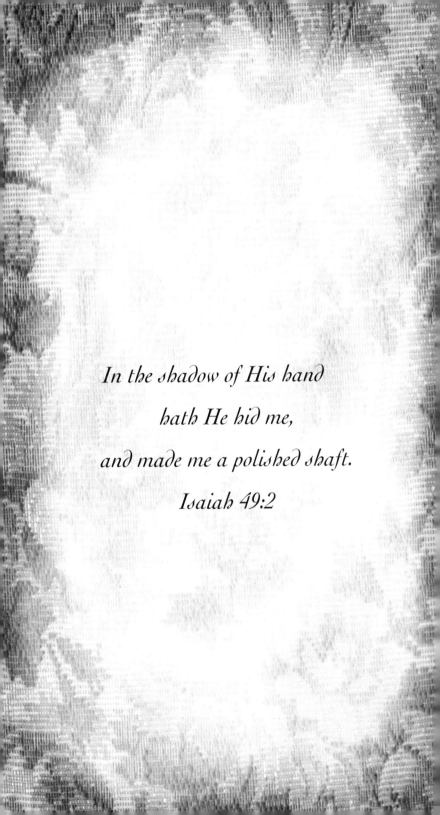

*In the shadow of His hand*

*hath He hid me,*

*and made me a polished shaft.*

*Isaiah 49:2*

# December, 1999
# Eureka, California

Many years of trusting and believing had brought me to this special moment. No one else in the room now, no adoring audience, no beloved companion...only my ever present Friend, watching and listening as I looked at myself in the bathroom mirror.

I gasped in disbelief as I clasped my chest. "No, Lord, it can't be." I stammered.

I stared in horror at the indentation on my breast. Denial wasn't an option. It was me...my body...not someone else's.

"Help me Jesus," I sobbed.

"This is just between you and me for now, Lord. I won't tell my mom and dad or my brother and sisters here in California. Not yet. I've got to get back home to Carroll. He's got to be the first to know."

"We've harmonized for 25 years now. We've shared the same bed, sung from hundreds of platforms, pastored a church, cried over the same heartaches, and shared a bundle of joys. Now we share again."

It happened to him eleven years ago...now will it happen to me? I whispered the dreaded word, "Cancer." The note it strikes is fear.

"I must hurry. I've got to get home. Carroll will be there and he will understand." My ever present help held me in his everlasting arms that night and carried me home to Kennett, Missouri.

I will go before thee, and make
the crooked places straight:
I will break in pieces
the gates of brass, and
cut in sunder the bars of iron.
And I will give thee
the treasures of darkness,
and hidden riches of secret places,
that thou mayest know that I,
the Lord, which call thee
by thy name,
am the God of Israel.
Isaiah 45:2-3

# Then There was God

Back home in Kennett…doctor's appointment made, a few tears shed, and then two phone calls of hope.

"Hello! This is Brother Freddie Clark. God has spoken to me and told me to give you a message. You are to cancel all your appointments and all your concerts, and stay in Kennett. God has told me to come to Kennett and have a healing service."

With grateful hearts, we scheduled the healing service for January 18th, the same day as my doctor's appointment.

Meanwhile, we told my troubling news to our families. Then the second call. This one was from my brother, John McDonald, in Eureka, California.

"Priscilla, I have a prophecy for you. It was given to me five years ago when Charles Pierce was preaching for me. He turned to me in the middle of one of his messages and spoke these words:

*"You're going to see one of your sisters — not that I wish it, not that I hope it — but God is going to slow her down. She and her husband are going to write some of the best songs they've ever written before. God's going to give them a rest and they're going to go back out more spiritual than they ever have been in all their lives. God's going to touch her and give her strength, because she's got to have strength. These are my children and I'm going to bring them to a place to anoint them to do what I've called them to do. Revival is going to spring from Kennett, Missouri."*

I could hardly imagine that this prophecy was given five years ago in the month of February, 1994. The messages coming from my body were dismaying, but the words from the Lord filled me with hope.

*Wherefore glorify ye
the Lord in the fires,
even the name of the
Lord God of Israel
in the isles of the sea.
Isaiah 24:15*

# New Territory

Remembering…

As a child I grew up in a powerful spiritual environment of faith. Every morning at 6:00, Dad would call each of us by name: "Janet, Joy, Beverly, John, Mary, Priscilla, (and later Julie)."

We knew it was the family hour of prayer, followed by a Bible study.

If we were sick, we went to church and we were prayed for. There was never an excuse good enough for missing a church service. It was a family priority.

Only once in my life do I remember my parents taking me to a doctor's office. That was a time when Dad and I had been sick for several days with the Hong Kong flu.

Although Dad was a very dedicated Christian, he had a way of making all our spiritual activities a lot of fun. He and mom taught us to love the work of God.

We believed God would heal us and He always did. We were a very healthy family.

Now the disease in my body would lead me down new paths. It seems I was chosen by God to be a witness to a host of doctors and nurses who would become a part of the unfolding miracle.

Isaiah 24:15 was to be my destination.

*Wherefore glorify ye the Lord in the fires, even the name of the Lord God of Israel in the isles of the sea.*

Today I wrote these words in my journal:

- *Glorify God in the fires of persecution by resolute adherence to the truth.*
- *Glorify God in the fires of temptation by a firm resistance to evil.*
- *Glorify God in the fires of affliction by patient submission to His will.*

*The McDonald clan: (clockwise from left) Priscilla, Joy, John, Janet, Mary, Dad, Mom, baby Julie, and Beverly*

*Priscilla and her Dad on the Sunday School bus.*

And the peace of God
which passes all understanding
shall keep your hearts and
minds through Christ Jesus.
Philippians 4:7

# No Hope?

Went to the doctor on January 18th and received the most negative report imaginable.

By this time, a large ugly tumor had appeared beneath the dimpled-in area on my breast.

It was about the size of a lemon and was daily becoming more unsightly.

The doctor examined me and then said, "I'm sorry, Mrs. McGruder, but you do have breast cancer. It appears to be in an advanced stage."

Needless to say, we were stunned. Carroll was the first to speak. "Doctor, we believe that life and death is in the hands of God, but from your experience, how much time do you think we have?"

"From my experience with cancer, I would think that your wife has two months to live. This cancer is in the fourth stage. If there were some possibility you could live for two more years, you really wouldn't want to because your body would be so deteriorated."

As I heard the doctor's words, immediately the words of Romans 8:28 spoke to me.

*For we know that all things work together for good to them that love God, to them who are the called according to His purpose.*

It was instantly obvious to me that good was destined to come out of this horrible news. God had given me His Word concerning the disease in my body. The nurses ran over to me and said, "Oh, Mrs. McGruder, we're so sorry."

I looked at the two nurses and the doctor and began testifying to them. The two nurses were visibly shaken and teary eyed.

Then I said to them, "In Hebrews, the Bible says that Jesus Christ is the same yesterday, today, and forever. Do you know that in 1988 God healed my husband of lymphoma cancer? I believe God's gonna do the same for me."

The nurses and doctor stared at me in wonder. Usually when a woman hears that she has two months to live, she either faints or goes into hysteria. And yet, here I was testifying to them that God was going to heal me.

Again God spoke to me. The words were from Philippians 4:7:

*And the peace of God which passes all understanding shall keep your hearts and minds through Christ Jesus.*

A powerful feeling came over me as I left the doctor's office that day. The terror had been replaced by a supernatural peace.

But thou, when thou prayest,
enter into thy closet,
and when thou hast shut thy door,
pray to thy Father
which is in secret; and
thy Father which seeth in secret
shall reward thee openly.
Matthew 6:6

# Angel Room

Returned to my prayer room again this morning.

For the days ahead, I needed an abundant infusion of power. My longtime habit of rising early and having an hour of communion with Jesus has always been my mainstay.

My time with God would now be my indispensable source of fortification for the pain I was about to endure.

Our home has a set of French doors that open into a small formal living room. The first piece of wall décor that I placed in that room was a guardian angel picture my mother gave me fifty years ago. It was the famous picture of two children crossing a precarious bridge under the watchful eyes of an unseen angel.

Now angels of every description fill the corners, tables, and shelves of the room. A golden harp occupies one corner with two cherubs flying above it. My angel room was destined to become my prayer room.

On one of the end tables I kept a Scripture box which I would draw from each morning. It provided a constant source of inspiration.

I purchased a red spiral notebook and began making daily entries of my journey with God during this time of great personal stress. Now, that journal has become a part of this book.

The journal entries begin like this:

**Monday...**

*God woke me up at 3:38 a.m. and I felt His presence so beautifully.....*

**Sunday...**

*At 8:00 a.m. I was lying on the floor in my angel room and I was very sick.....*

**Tuesday...**

*I awoke at 3:30 a.m. Went to my prayer room and began praising the Lord.....*

**Thursday...**

*Arose at 4:30 a.m. and had sweet communion with the Lord.....*

My angel room became holy ground—a place where I took giant strides in my walk with God. The time we spent together in that room is a priceless treasure that I will carry with me forever.

Each morning I knelt by the couch to pray.

When I had no strength to kneel, I would lie on the floor and pour out my heart to God. Now there is a worn spot on the carpet where I knelt. The couch has a large spot that has been discolored by my tears.

From time to time, friends who step into that room will say, "I feel such peace in this place." I nod knowingly.

My angel room...my prayer room...a place where I wrestled and prevailed.

*Early morning in the angel room*

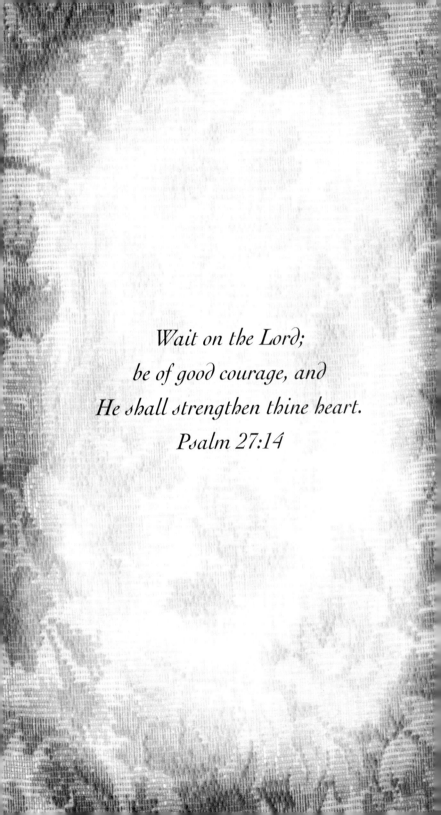

*Wait on the Lord;*
*be of good courage, and*
*He shall strengthen thine heart.*
*Psalm 27:14*

# In the Waiting Room

The night of January 18th…went to the healing service at church.

Brother Clark and the saints anointed me with oil in the name of Jesus and prayed for me. Nothing sensational happened. Even though I felt nothing special, I decided I would just stand on God's Word.

"That cancer has turned to a stone," Brother Clark said to me. "Go ahead and get it cut out of your body."

The next day I went to the hospital for a mammogram test and then to Dr. Kakaya to get a biopsy. Carroll and my sister, Mary Wilson, accompanied me.

A strange thing happened as the doctor tried to extract a piece of tissue for the biopsy. He tried three times and still was unsuccessful. The doctor's long needle broke in the middle of the procedure. He was sweating profusely and there was a lot of blood. Carroll nearly passed out. Mary and I managed to hold steady.

The doctor kept saying, "It's so hard that it won't come out. It's like a rock." He asked for some stronger instruments. Finally he was able to get the tissue that he needed for the biopsy.

A day later it was back to the hospital for an ultra sound, bone scan tests, and blood work. Again the news was not good. The ultra sound test showed a spot on my left rib cage and spots on my stomach.

I was told to go across the street to Dr. Kakaya to get the reports read. When I approached the door, I was stunned to see the sign on the door: "Closed until Monday." That gave me four days of waiting!

The words of Psalm 27:14 became my strength for those days.

*Wait on the Lord; be of good courage, and He shall strengthen thine heart.*

Meanwhile, Satan was using all these negative reports to wear at my mind. "You're going to die. Right now that cancer is spreading through your body. It's in your stomach. It's moving through your body. Your mother died of cervical cancer, your uncle died of cancer, your cousin had cancer, and now you. You're going to die." Satan was trying his best to wear me down.

That night as I tossed in my bed, I repeated over and over again the Scriptures that the Lord had given me. Again God was there and peace prevailed.

When God asks us to wait, it is not because he's being mean or because he's wasting time. He's doing a great work while we're waiting. He's conforming us into the image of Christ and that takes time.

Some people say, "No good could come out of this. This can't be God." But these trials are designed to make us and not to destroy us. It is permitted by God to mold us into the image of his son and not to disfigure us for life.

He is not testing us to see if we'll fail, but to show us how strong we really are. We don't need to try to manipulate our situation or maneuver our way out of it. God asks us to allow that trial to accomplish what He intended in our lives.

*Trust in the Lord and do good.*

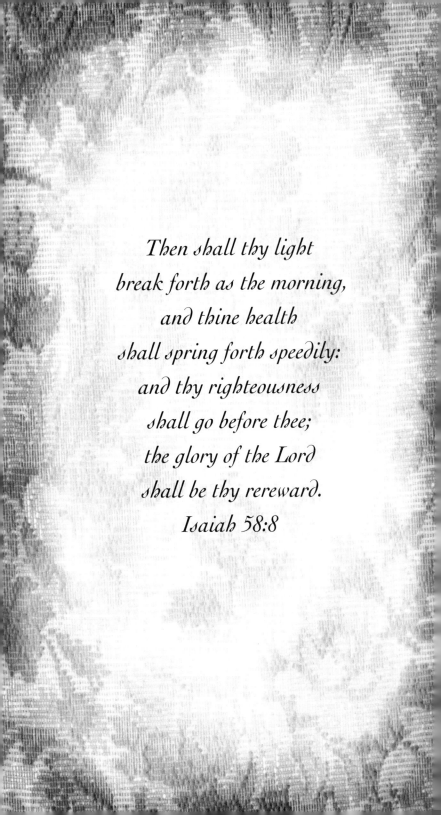

Then shall thy light
break forth as the morning,
and thine health
shall spring forth speedily:
and thy righteousness
shall go before thee;
the glory of the Lord
shall be thy rereward.

Isaiah 58:8

# Day Star

Still waiting. I awoke at 5:30 a.m. and walked into the family room. As I looked out the window, I saw the brightest star I have ever seen. It seemed as if it was lighting up the whole yard. I realized that a star shining at 5:30 a.m. was a most unusual happening.

As I watched the miraculous star, the Word of the Lord in Isaiah 58:8 came to me.

> *Then shall thy light break forth as the morning, and thine health shall spring forth speedily: and thy righteousness shall go before thee; the glory of the Lord shall be they rereward.*

Then God led me to Isaiah 43:2.

> *When thou passest through the waters I will be with thee, and through the rivers, they*

*shall not overflow thee; when thou walkest through the fire, thou shall not be burned neither shall the flame kindle upon thee.*

God's light filled my heart and gave me strength for another day of waiting.

Peace I leave with you,
my peace I give unto you:
not as the world giveth,
give I unto you.
Let not your heart be troubled,
neither let it be afraid.
John 14:27

# A Mother's Prayers

Still waiting.

I woke up at 4:00 a.m. and had sweet communion with the Lord. Then came a call I will never forget. It was from Melba Vincent, a longtime family friend from Louisiana. What a welcome voice.

"While I was praying for you today, Priscilla, God spoke to me and reminded me of something. Years ago when you were only a child, your mother prayed a prayer for you. She asked God to sustain you because she saw something special in you."

The words spoken about my mom brought back treasured memories. My mother was the preacher in the family and had been a great source of spiritual strength to me. I had thought of her many times during the past several weeks, and had often wished she could be with me during this time of sickness.

I was deeply moved when I heard Melba speak these words: "Priscilla, your mother's prayers never die."

I began weeping and praising God. Melba and I spoke in tongues as we prayed, bound together in the spirit across the many miles that separated us.

My soul was saturated by the presence of God and somehow the waiting didn't seem so long.

*Baby Priscilla and her Mother*

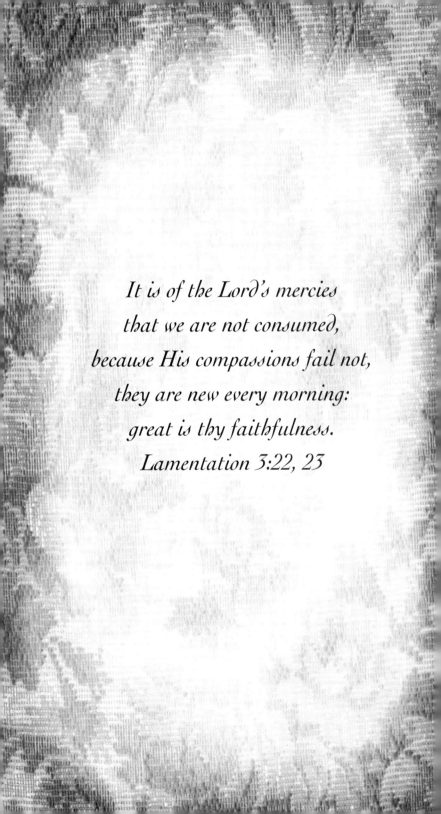

*It is of the Lord's mercies*
*that we are not consumed,*
*because His compassions fail not,*
*they are new every morning:*
*great is thy faithfulness.*
*Lamentation 3:22, 23*

# Finally

January 26, 2000. Monday had finally arrived. Back to the doctor's office to hear his report.

Even the negative news was good! "Mrs, McGruder, those spots on your rib cage and stomach?"

"Yes doctor, what are they? Has the cancer spread?"

"No, no. They are only spots. Before you went in for your tests, we gave you some dye to swallow. Those spots on the x-ray are from the dye we gave you.

My mourning turned to laughter. Inside I was saying: "In your face, devil. In your face!"

"I believe the cancer is contained in your right breast." The doctor continued. "We will need to do a radical mastectomy immediately. Now, you are a small framed woman, Mrs. McGruder, so there is a good chance we will have to graft some skin from your hip to your chest."

I had heard so many negative things about skin grafts that I began to pray a rather childish prayer: "Lord stretch that skin so they won't have to do a graft."

The next day I went in for surgery. The Word from the Lord was contained in four simple words: *Great is thy faithfulness*. I knew I was in capable hands.

When I came out of the anesthesia and spoke with the doctor, the first thing he said was, "We were able to stretch the skin and it wasn't necessary to do the skin graft."

"Thank you, Jesus!" I rejoiced.

Carroll grinned and said, "It only stands to reason. She didn't want to wear her hip on her chest." Again I was laughing.

"Tell me about the cancer, doctor," I persisted.

"I've been doing this kind of surgery for twenty-five years now. I've only seen this happen two times–once in India and once in New York." The doctor informed me. "Your body went to war against that cancer and the cancer became encapsulated in a tissue. Mrs. McGruder, the cancerous tissue turned into a stone!"

*For the Lord God is a*
*sun and shield:*
*the Lord will give*
*grace and glory:*
*no good thing will He*
*withhold from them*
*that walk uprightly.*
*Psalm 84:11*

# Uninsured

"So, Mr. & Mrs. McGruder, what kind of insurance do you have?"

"Sorry," we replied, "We have none."

"How do you plan to pay for your surgery and treatments?"

"We're not sure," Carroll answered, "but we will pay. We can assure you of that."

"We have a policy here that if every bill is paid on or before the due date, the amount of the bill will be reduced by one third."

"Then we will pay every bill on or before the due date," my husband stated.

"When we were getting in the car that day, I asked, "Carroll, how will we pay? Do we have the money?"

"No, we don't. We have about $3000 in the bank and that's all."

"That won't begin to touch our costs, will it?" I questioned with a worried note in my voice.

"Let's agree on one thing, Priscilla," was Carroll's reply. "You concentrate on getting well and I'll concentrate on paying the bills."

"Sounds good to me," I answered. And that's what we did.

The first bill that arrived was for $21,000 and it was due the following Monday. On Monday morning Carroll dressed and prepared to leave the house.

"Where are you going?" Mary and I queried.

"I'm going to pay the hospital bill," he answered.

"Do you have the money?" we asked.

"No, but I'm going to the post office to get it," came the reply. "God is going to give us a miracle."

"Can we go with you?" we asked excitedly.

"Yes, you may go on one condition. You must promise me you will stay in the car."

"Why can't we go in with you?"

"Because they don't allow revival services in government offices. We can't have you shouting and dancing in the post office." We agreed to stay in the car.

The three of us jumped into the car and headed for the post office in a great spirit of expectation. Carroll's faith was contagious.

He went inside and came out with a big stack of mail. Most of them were get well cards and letters from concerned people. God seemed to direct him as to which envelopes he should open first. The first card read:

*I know you are undergoing
surgery. We want to be of help.*

Inside the card was a check for $2000. We began our rejoicing. The next card said:

*We're praying for you. We believe
God is going to see you through.*

The card contained a check for $1000. Another note simply read:

*Just wanted to be a blessing.*

Enclosed was a check for $500. Another card read like this:

*I was praying today and God told me
that with surgery and recovery and
the expenses involved, you would
need some people to stand with you.
We believe in your ministry and
we've been blessed by it. God told me
that today when you get this letter,
this is the amount you would need.*

We gasped in amazement as we looked at a check for $18,000. The revival service took place inside the car. On that day, the sum of the checks sent to the church in our behalf totaled $21,500.

The miracle continued. We never had the money in advance, but every time there was a bill due, God would graciously send the money that very week.

When the cancer came, immediately we were forced to lay off all our singers, musicians, and technicians. One of them, Mark Dollins, came to us and said, "I have some invitations to sing and speak in various places. If it wouldn't embarrass you, I would like to turn these services into fund raisers to help pay Sis. McGruder's bills."

Though he had never preached a revival before or sung publicly on his own, he returned and presented our church with $10,000 in behalf of our medical expenses.

Over and over, God provided. The total bill was over $100,000. All of the money was channeled to our church to help us in time of need. Every bill was paid on time.

We found that God pays much better than an insurance policy. Not 80% or 50%. He pays it all!

*A friend loveth at all times*
*and a brother is born*
*for adversity.*
*Proverbs 17:17*

# Encouragers

So much to praise God for...

His healing in my body was greatly enhanced by the many encouragers He brought my way. I was surrounded daily by people who spoke their faith and not their fears. Negative thinking is a drain on the body and soul.

After my first cancer diagnosis, Carroll began calling our family. One of the first calls he made was to my sister, Mary Wilson in Sacramento, California. Mary and I were very close both in age and in spirit.

Amazingly, within two hours of the call, Mary and her two daughters and my youngest sister, Julie were on an airplane headed for St. Louis. They rented a car in St. Louis and drove through the night to Kennett. My heart overflowed when I saw them pull into our driveway the next morning.

Mary stayed with me 24-7 for the next three months. Sometimes in the middle of the darkest night, she just laid by my side and held my hand. She was a witness to many of the events recorded in this book.

Her husband, Nathaniel Wilson, would fly in from time to time. He was so kind to let Mary stay with me. The Rock Church in Sacramento likewise gave me much prayer support and many acts of kindness.

My sisters each came to be with me for several weeks and each one contributed her unique talents towards helping us.

The ladies from our church in Kennett were phenomenal. Every day they came to the house and brought food. They would set the table and have everything totally ready for us. Their practical love buoyed my spirits daily.

Our children and grandchildren surrounded us with love and affection. At first our granddaughter, Prisda, could not understand why "Nana" could not hold her. Instead she would just come and stand beside me wherever I was sitting.

The mailbox provided another source of refreshing. Hundreds of cards and letters arrived from all over the world, some from people we had never met. Many people would send an encouraging Bible verse in their correspondence. Invariably, the verse that was sent would be the exact word I needed for the day.

Every room of our house was filled with beautiful flowers that were sent to me from all over the country.

Other people gave gifts of finance and became a valuable part of my healing miracle. The phone calls and visits regularly provided the strength I needed for the day.

Two of my dearest friends Mignon Adams and Melba Vincent called me every week with a fresh word from the Lord.

I will always be grateful for the network of support given to Carroll and me. Each encouragement taught me something. I am forever committed. In the future, I too will be one of God's best encouragers.

Thank you God for teaching me about compassion. It was one of the most important facets of your character and your ministry. Now it will be part of mine.

Behold I have created the smith
that bloweth the coals of fire,
and that bringeth forth an
instrument for his work.
Isaiah 54:16

# Be Still

Went to the doctor on January 31st and he removed my drainage tubes.

At the time of the mastectomy, he had removed fourteen lymph nodes. He reported that they had been tested and six of them were malignant. Then he advised me that I needed to have a series of chemotherapy treatments to rid my body of any remaining cancer cells.

The treatments would begin in March and end in August. I would be scheduled for one treatment each month. My assignment for February was to be still and recuperate my strength.

After the hectic month of January, now I was being told to be still and rest. A month of sitting still was not an easy task for someone like me. I read in my morning devotions from Isaiah 30:7. Concerning the Egyptians the Lord said,

*Their strength is to sit still.*

"In order to really know God, inward stillness is absolutely necessary. Quiet tension is not trust. It is simply compressed anxiety. To stand still is but to renew strength for some greater advance in due time."*

*Stand still and see the salvation of the Lord. Exodus 14:13*

My sister, Joy Haney, called and gave me two inspiring Scriptures.

*Behold I have created the smith that bloweth the coals on the fire, and that bringeth forth an instrument for His work.*
*Isaiah 54:16*

"God tells us that even the power to do hurt comes from God. Don't be afraid. God controls the power, even over those things that could harm you."

As we were talking on the phone, God gave Joy this Scripture from Isaiah 31:5. She inserted my name in the verse.

*As birds flying, so will the Lord of hosts defend Priscilla, defending also He will deliver Priscilla, and passing over, He will preserve Priscilla.*

Wow! God was doing so many wonderful things for me during this time of stillness.

---

* Cowman, Mrs. Chas. E., Streams in the Desert (Los Angeles, CA: Cowman Publications Inc., 1960) p. 121

*I will go before thee,*
*and make the crooked*
*places straight:*
*I will break in pieces*
*the gates of brass,*
*and cut in sunder*
*the bars of iron.*
*Isaiah 45:2*

# How Sweet It Is!

February 13th was a good day. I would be able to go back to church for the first time since my operation. I could hardly wait.

From a child, my parents had made Sundays very exciting days for me. They taught me to love the house of God. Our family was totally involved in God's work, and Sunday was the busiest day of all.

I will always remember the Sundays of my childhood. Dad drove the church bus. He would take us with him on his Sunday School route and the ride was always fun. (Dad kept driving that bus over the years. Two years ago, he took me on his bus route once again and I loved it!)

After church we went to sing for the radio broadcast. Then we would all go out for dinner. In those days, very few families could afford to eat at restaurants, but Sunday was such a busy day, that my dad did this to help my mother.

At three we went to prayer meeting, then on to the nursing home at four. At six, mom and dad conducted children's church, and this was followed by the evening evangelistic service.

Missing church was never an option for us. As I anticipated the morning service, God gave me this scripture found in Isaiah 45:2:

*I will go before thee, and make the crooked places straight: I will break in pieces the gates of brass, and cut in sunder the bars of iron:*

I wrote these words in my journal:

***God will remove all the obstacles and hindrances out of the paths of those who are called of God or who are trying to do a work for Him. Obstacles should never be a hindrance to us. There is hardly anything in life worth doing, that is not difficult. A way will always open for the obedient, resolute, and trustful child of God. God has set me apart as an instrument to perform an important public service in the name of Jehovah.***

With that inspiration, I went to church. The privilege seemed sweeter than it ever had before.

I may face things tomorrow
I can't comprehend today.
Circumstances so uncertain
Make it hard to find the strength
to pray;
But I'm living in the promise,
I'll never leave you,
I will always see you through;
So what's this mountain to an
eagle flying high
From heaven's point of view.

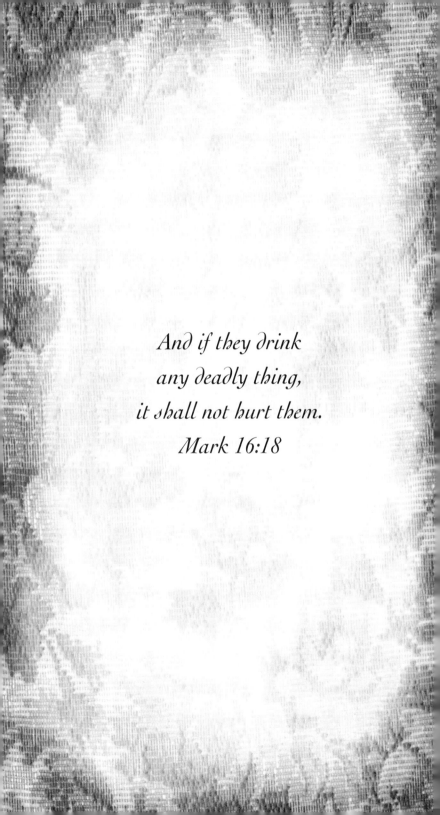

*And if they drink
any deadly thing,
it shall not hurt them.*
*Mark 16:18*

# Chemotherapy

March arrived. Time for my first chemo treatments.

God sent another blessing in the form of Dr. Bertram, who had just moved to the bootheel of Missouri. The doctor was trained at Johns Hopkins University in Baltimore. He had been the head of the department of breast cancer at UCLA for twenty years. When he moved to Missouri he planned to retire from medicine, but then he said, "In this area there are so many women with cancer, I need to try to help them." Dr. Bertram decided to temporarily come out of retirement.

And so it was that God provided me with one of the finest specialists in the country, without having to leave home. I believe God wanted me to stay right here in Missouri so I could be a witness in my home town of Kennett and the surrounding area.

I woke up early on the day of my first treatment. As was my daily custom, I went to the local gym to walk. While I was circling the gym, I began praising God for all the prayers He had answered thus far.

"Thank you God for bringing me through my mastectomy, thank you for stretching my skin, thank you for giving me peace. Now Lord, as you know, I'm having my first chemotherapy treatment today. I don't know what I'm going to face, but I know you're going to be with me.

Immediately the word of the Lord came to me. It was a verse found in Mark 16:18.

*If they drink any deadly thing, it shall not hurt them.*

It immediately occurred to me what the Lord was telling me. When you take chemotherapy, you are taking poison into your body to kill the poison that is already there. God was reassuring me that the poison from the chemotherapy would not harm me.

When the word of the Lord came to me, I began leaping and running around that gym rejoicing. There was no one there but me and the Lord—no prayer group, no pastor, no husband. Just me and Him. Didn't Jesus say that one could put to flight a thousand?

I was so thrilled by the word the Lord had given me that I was actually anxious for my treatment to begin. When I got to the hospital the nurse looked at me with a puzzled expression and asked, "Why are you so happy?"

When I told her about my experience in the gym, she just looked at me quizzically as if to say, "We've really got one on our hands this time. This one's gonna be a doozy."

God kept His word and helped me through every treatment.

When I went for my treatment in April, the nurse said to me, "Your blood count is high. You must be doing something right."

"Oh no," I answered. "It's not me doing it. It's my God."

While I was receiving my treatment in May, the nurse hooked me up and then left the room. This time, however, I observed that she put the needle into a smaller vein than the one she usually used. As I looked down at my arm, I noticed a rash had broken out from my wrist to my elbow. It was red and it was itching.

I remembered from my husband's chemotherapy, that if the chemo gets out of the vein, it can burn your body badly.

The accuser began his diatribe: "See there, your body is going to get burned. Where is your God now? You heard his word when he said if you drink any deadly thing it wouldn't hurt you. You danced and shouted around the gym. Look at you now."

I answered him boldly. "My God's right here. He told me if I drink any deadly thing it wouldn't hurt me. My God always keeps His word."

I looked at that rash and I said to myself, "I've got a choice. I can either give myself over to fear or I can believe God. I choose to believe God's Word."

About that time, the nurse came back in the room. "You need to take a look at this," I said to her. "I think something's wrong."

When she saw what was happening, she got pretty shook up. She cleansed the opening in my arm and then changed the needle to another vein.

"Don't worry about it," I reassured her. "My God's watching over me and everything's gonna be all right."

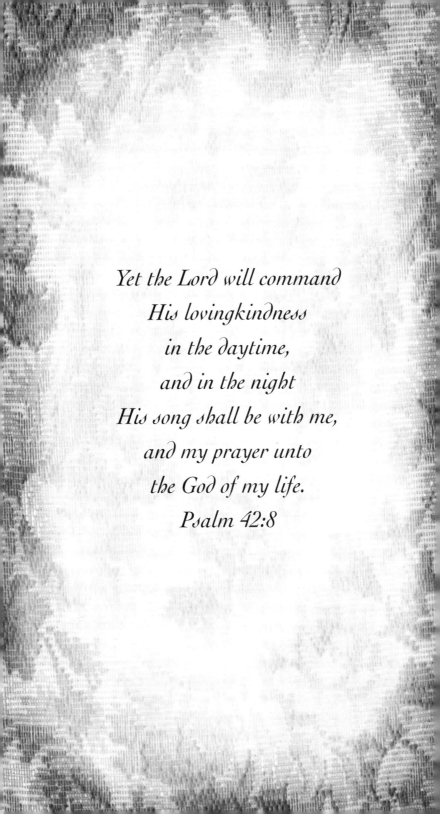

*Yet the Lord will command*
*His lovingkindness*
*in the daytime,*
*and in the night*
*His song shall be with me,*
*and my prayer unto*
*the God of my life.*
*Psalm 42:8*

# Night Seasons

Arrived in June for my fourth treatment. I was told that my dosage would be increased considerably.

After that treatment, I went home and tried to go to bed. My body was shaking all over. I went to the family room and laid on the couch. That didn't work. So I went to the lounge chair, but that was no good. Finally, I laid on the floor, just shaking from my head to my toes. It was definitely a night season.

And then came the song…

*You can have a song in your heart in the night;*
*After every trial, after every mile.*
*Anyone can sing when the sun's shining bright,*
*But you need a song in your heart at night.*

Once again God spoke to me through His word. First He gave me Psalm 42:8:

*Yet the Lord will command His lov-ingkindness in the daytime, and in the night His song shall be with me, and my prayer unto the God of my life.*

Then He gave me Zachariah 2:10.

*Sing and rejoice, O daughter of Zion: for, lo, I come, and I will dwell in the midst of thee, saith the Lord.*

Finally He led me to Isaiah 30:29.

*Ye shall have a song, as in the night when a holy solemnity is kept; and gladness of heart, as when one goeth with a pipe to come into the mountain of the Lord, to the mighty One of Israel.*

There on the floor, in the middle of a long night, I found the mighty One of Israel and He ministered hope to me.

We can't lie down and give up when we are weak. We've got to fight the good fight until the battle's won. Through my battle, I have come to believe that God loves us too much to shield us from everything that is uncomfortable. But in the night season, He will always be there to help you find your song again.

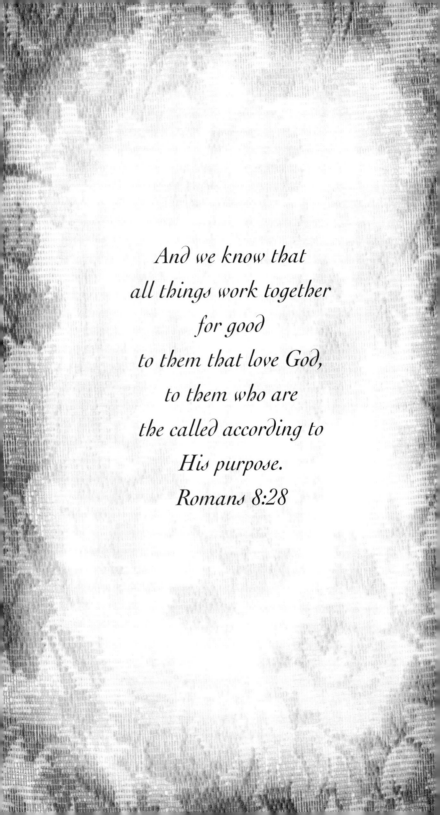

*And we know that
all things work together
for good
to them that love God,
to them who are
the called according to
His purpose.
Romans 8:28*

# A Bad Hair Day

"Lord, I know that most people who go through chemotherapy lose their hair. But I'm asking you to let me keep mine."

"It'll be okay, Priscilla," my husband said. "It's really not so bad."

"Maybe it's not so bad for a man, but for a woman it's terrible. My hair is my covering. It's my glory," I retorted.

"If you lose your hair, I'll be your covering," Carroll tried to reassure me.

"Well I've asked God to let me keep my hair and I think He will, but…if I should lose it, I don't want it to happen when anyone is with me except you. I've heard so many stories about this. Wouldn't it be awful if my hair came out while I was playing the organ at church? No! And I don't want my children or my grandchildren to be there to see me if I do lose my hair."

During my bout with cancer, I had plenty of time for thinking and reminiscing. Years ago before I was even born, there was a bad hair day that forever determined the direction of my life.

My Dad was a part of the clean up crew that went to Pearl Harbor right after the bombing. While he was there, he was greatly disturbed by all the death and destruction he witnessed. He was so upset, that he began to pray: "Lord, if you'll bring me home safely, I'll give my life to you."

God brought him home safely, but he did nothing about his promise to the Lord.

One day my mother asked my sister, Janet, to ask the blessing on the food. Janet began praying, "Thank you God for bringing my daddy home safely from the war…"

When she said those words, Dad was smitten in his heart as he remembered the promise he had made to God. He began to weep.

Dad immediately began making plans to go to church the following Sunday. He decided to take us to a beautiful Methodist Church in downtown Modesto.

Sunday morning came, and mom was having a terrible time getting the three girls (Janet, Joy, and Beverly) ready for church. It seems all the women in the family were having a bad hair day.

It kept getting later and later. Soon it became apparent that we were going to be late for church.

Finally Mom suggested, "We've gone to this much trouble to get ready, but it's really getting late. Why don't we just go to the little church up the street?"

And so it was that the McDonald family walked into a Pentecostal Church for the first time in their lives. Brother Rode was the pastor and the church was in the middle of a red hot revival service. My mom and dad were deeply touched as they witnessed the power of God. They came back to the Sunday night service. That night they repented of their sins at an old fashioned altar of prayer. They were baptized in Jesus name and filled with the Holy Ghost. Their lives were never the same.

The following Friday night, they attended a rally service. When they walked in the door, their pastor, Brother Rode, said, "Here come my brand new babies. Give us your testimony, Brother McDonald."

My Dad had no idea how to give a proper testimony. So with great sincerity he burst out: "Hot diggity dog for Jesus!" and then did a somersault down the aisle.

Now if the Lord could turn a bad hair day into the blessing of a lifetime, perhaps he would answer my simple request.

Although God chose not to answer my original request, He was, nevertheless, merciful to me. I was alone in my bathroom when I let out a frantic squeal. The drain to our shower was clogged with hair and water was running onto the floor. As I reached up to rub the top of my head, a big clump of hair came out in my hand.

By that time, Carroll had run into the bathroom and was looking at me. Tears were streaming down my face as I looked in the mirror. He took the brush and brushed until I was totally slick. Not a hair on my head.

Then he grinned and said, "Priscilla, you're the most beautiful bald headed woman I've ever seen in my life."

Through my tears, I began to laugh. Then we both sat on the floor of the bathroom laughing while we passed the mirror back and forth to each other.

My sister Mary, took me to Cape Girardeau and bought me a beautiful wig made out of human hair. It was very expensive.

Somehow I never felt comfortable wearing the wig, even though it was the same color my hair had been. It was very heavy and it just wasn't me. So Carroll took me out and we bought hats—lots of them in every color imaginable.

News traveled fast. When I arrived at church that Sunday I was wearing a pretty black hat. As I entered the sanctuary, I was delighted to see that almost all the women in the church were wearing hats. One man came with his head shaved, so I would not feel alone. What love and gratitude I felt in my heart as I worshiped God that day.

It was apparent to me—when you're in God's hands, bad hair days can be a blessing from the Lord.

# Hair Stages

*Holly and Priscilla*

*Mary and Priscilla*

*Priscilla and Carroll*

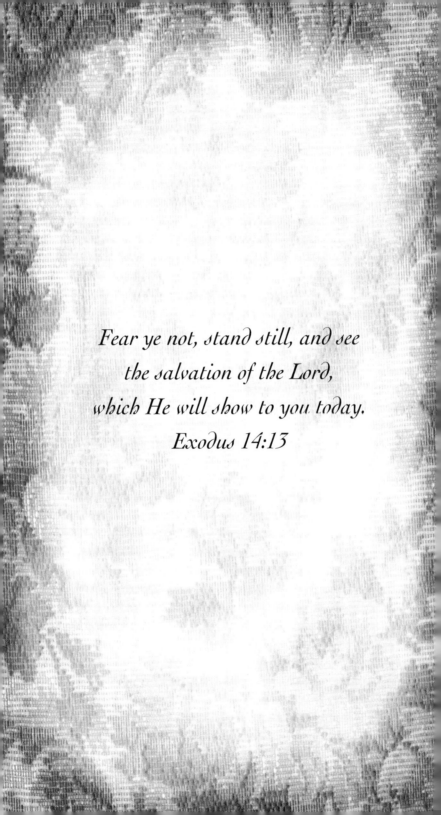

*Fear ye not, stand still, and see*
*the salvation of the Lord,*
*which He will show to you today.*
*Exodus 14:13*

# Still Standing

Awoke in the wee hours of the morning, my body racked with pain.

I slipped out of bed as quietly as I could and staggered toward my prayer room. But when I walked into the room I realized I was too sick to pray or to read my Bible.

Carroll also awoke and sensed that something was wrong. He got out of bed and went to find me. He located me in the prayer room. I was in my nightgown, looking very disheveled.

As he entered the prayer room, he was shocked to see me standing on my Bible. His first thought was, "Oh, no! Priscilla's mind has snapped."

He came to me and I fell over on him.

"What's wrong, Priscilla?" he questioned me fearfully.

"Oh Carroll, I'm so sick. I can't pray or read my Bible. All I could think to do was to stand here on the Word."

Carroll held me in his arms and prayed for me as I remained there—simply standing on the Word.

In retrospect, it seems to be the best thing I could have done. When there's nothing left to do, just keep standing. Stand on God's promises. Stand on what you know is true.

*Stand still and see the salvation of the Lord.*

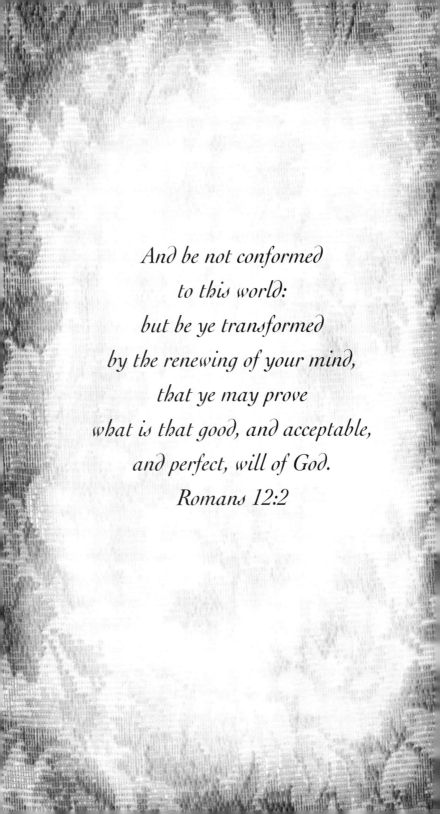

And be not conformed
to this world:
but be ye transformed
by the renewing of your mind,
that ye may prove
what is that good, and acceptable,
and perfect, will of God.
Romans 12:2

# Too Good to be True, But It Is!

I am blessed.

God has given me a husband of great emotional strength. When going through a serious sickness, it is important that you are surrounded by people who are positive in their outlook.

Carroll's constant support made my struggle more bearable. What a blessing to have someone who kept his sense of humor through it all. He always knew how to make me laugh, sometimes at the most strenuous moments.

I married Carroll when I was twenty-seven years old. He had experienced the loss of his first wife as a result of an automobile accident. She had been killed instantly.

I, on the other hand, had turned down all my previous suitors, quite sure that I had not yet met the person who would be God's perfect will for my life. Mom always taught us that there is a permissive will of God, but that it is best to find the perfect will of God.

After the death of Carroll's wife, people located in various parts of the country had approached him and said: "I know a woman who would make a wonderful companion for you. Her name is Priscilla McDonald. She works for the Pentecostal Publishing House in St. Louis, Missouri. Why don't you find a way to meet her?"

Someone sent him a record I had made. When he saw my picture on the cover and listened to me sing he said, "That's my wife. Whether she marries me or not, that's my wife and I love her already."

He called me on the phone. The conversation went something like this.

"Priscilla McDonald? My name is Carroll McGruder. I am the pastor of a church in Twin Falls, Idaho. I would like to invite you to fly out to our church and sing for us. I won't try to be subtle about this. The truth is that many people have come to me and told me that I need to meet you. I lost my wife several months ago in a terrible automobile accident. I have prayed about this and decided that I would like to meet you. Would you consider coming?"

"I'll have to think about it," was my reply. After seeking counsel from some of my trusted friends, I decided to accept the invitation.

I remember well that visit when I met Carroll for the very first time. From day one I knew that I loved him, and it was apparent that he felt the same way about me.

It was important to Carroll that he would find a good mother for his two children, Shawnee and Eric. Soon after I arrived, four year old Shawnee asked me to take her to the bathroom. While we were in there, I began to brush her hair. She looked up at me with her big blue eyes and said, "My mommy is dead."

Carroll sat in stunned silence when he heard the words as he was sitting in an adjoining room. Then he heard my answer. "My mommy died too. It's hard, but with the help of the Lord, we can get through this together." It was a moment to remember. He wiped a tear from his eye and was reassured that all would be well.

Before I left that week-end, I called my boss, Brother Agnew, in St. Louis to give him my two weeks notice. We were soon married and I moved to Twin Falls, Idaho for the next four years of my life.

Some days it seemed like a fairy-tale romance. But the real test of the marriage came through our struggles.

I walked with him through his bout with cancer in 1988. When my cancer came twelve years later, inwardly he was filled with terror. His first thoughts were, "Oh, no! Not again. I've already watched my first wife die, now will I have to lose Priscilla too?"

After our first doctor's appointment, we were sitting in the car getting ready to go home. He took me in his arms and said, "Priscilla, I love you, and I want you to know something. If this thing can be whipped, we're gonna whip it. But if two months is all we have, we're going to treat that two months with the most dignity we've ever shown. Our lives will be a statement for the world to see that there's no tragedy in dying in the faith."

Carroll was divinely prepared to walk through my night season with me and he did it with courage. He went to every doctor's appointment with me and was there for each operation as well as my chemotherapy.

What kept our marriage strong?  I believe it was because we had an open and honest relationship. In Carroll's words, "It's not bad to be honest, it's only bad to be rude. Priscilla is no less a lady to me now and no less desirable than she's ever been."

The doctor informed me, "It is possible that you can have reconstructive surgery."

Carroll's reply was, "It's your decision. If you do it, don't do it for me. I love you more now than I ever have. If you choose to do it, do it for yourself."

I did not choose to have the surgery.

One of the songs God gave Carroll, sums it all up. *It's Too Good to be True, But It Is!*

# Wedding Album

*The Lord knoweth
the days of the upright:
and their inheritance
shall be for ever.
Psalm 37:18*

# Family

Telling the children about my cancer was hard.

After Carroll and I married, I immediately assumed the awesome task of being a mother to Eric and Shawnee. The bond between us became stronger with each passing year.

Two years later, God added to our family of four. On February 15, 1979, I gave birth to a lovely baby girl. We named her Holly Elaine.

One of our most difficult tasks was to tell these three—Eric, Shawnee, and Holly—that their mother had breast cancer.

At the time, Holly was away from home, attending Southeast Missouri State College in Cape Girardeau.

Eric had married Michelle and they were the parents of two boys, Spencer and Jacob. Shawnee was married to Tim Trowbridge and they had given us two little granddaughters, Prisda and Taryn.

After the doctor gave us his negative diagnosis, Carroll broke the news to our adult children: "Your mother has cancer."

Everyone was stunned. Lots of questions and discussion followed the shocking news. Our children were doing their best to keep their composure, but I could see the terror in their eyes.

Eric and Shawnee had experienced the death of their first mother. They could only wonder if it was about to happen a second time.

Now they would journey with me through operations, chemotherapy treatments, and personal pain. We were a family and our love would soon be put to the test.

The first reaction of Shawnee, was intense anger and fear. She vented her anger to God in her prayers. "Why would God allow my mother to suffer so much pain? Is my mother going to die? How can we live without her?"

At the time of the diagnosis, Eric was ministering in Haiti. After the news came, he spent the day alone in the home where he was staying. Throughout the day, he prayed and committed his fears to the Lord. He left Haiti with a firm assurance that God was in control.

Eric and Shawnee and their families stayed very close to us that year.

Holly, however, was the one who suffered the most. "How could God allow this to happen to my mother?" she screamed when she heard the news. Separated from the family and living outside the confines of the home, provided the backdrop for the worst case scenario. Holly turned to alcohol and hard core drugs. It was more devastating to me than any pain that was in my body.

God spoke to me and said, "Leave her in my hands," and that's what I did. I gathered some stones and went to my prayer room. There I built an altar for Holly. I put her picture on top of it. and everyday I gave her to God.

We have watched Holly come back from a terrible pit of despair. In 2002, she enrolled in Teen Challenge, a Christian intervention program which has helped her escape the dreadful addictions in her life. God continues His work in Holly.

Shawnee now says, "I am ashamed that my faith was so weak. Through it all my mother was incredibly strong. I'd see people stop her in the stores and question her about her health. She'd give them a big smile and say, 'God's working a miracle in me.' She never wavered."

"I spent every moment I could with mom and dad. I wanted my children to be near them as much as possible. They are the role models I want my children to copy."

During this time, Shawnee began teaching her children to pray. It was beautiful to hear their heartfelt prayers for their 'Nana.' Spencer and Jacob likewise prayed every day for their 'Nana.'

In retrospect, I now see that not only was God working a miracle in me, but in His own sovereign way, He worked a miracle in each of us. We will never be the same.

*Our family*

Soon I'll soar like an eagle
High on wings of grace
High above the heavens
'Til I can almost see God's face
Rising in His splendor
To heights I never knew
What once looked like a mountain's
Just a hill
From heaven's point of view.

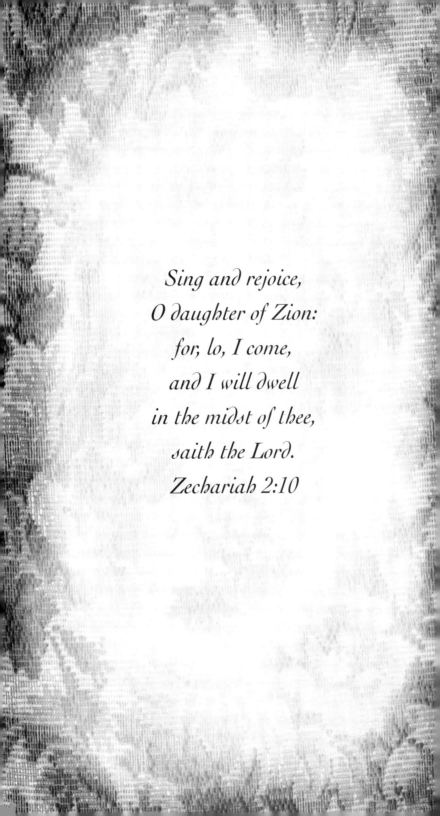

*Sing and rejoice,*
*O daughter of Zion:*
*for, lo, I come,*
*and I will dwell*
*in the midst of thee,*
*saith the Lord.*
*Zechariah 2:10*

# Let the Music Begin

Cancer put our music ministry on temporary hold.

Music has been an intricate part of the McGruders' lives. Carroll and I both began singing when we were very young.

Up through January, 2000, God has helped us produce seven record albums, thirty cassette tapes, fifteen CD's, and four videos. We have sung from 100's of platforms to many different types of people. Carroll is the gifted song writer in the family. He has a published portfolio of over three hundred songs, many of which have become chart songs.

When we first began traveling and singing, I made a serious promise to God. "Lord I will never sing in front of an audience anywhere until I have prayed at least one hour. I also promise you that whenever I sing, regardless of who I am singing to, I will always worship you with all my heart." By God's grace, I have always kept those two promises.

Now our music ministry came to an abrupt halt. In January, we cancelled all our concerts that were scheduled for the coming months. No more traveling, no more recording, no more concerts.

I held on to the prophecy that told us God was going to slow us down, and then He would restore our ministry as never before.

From January until my last treatment in August, we made no musical appearances. We laid off all our musicians and singers that traveled with us. I totally concentrated on my recovery.

We scheduled our first appointment to sing after my final chemotherapy treatment in August. We traveled to the Missouri District Camp Meeting of the United Pentecostal Church held in Arnold, Missouri. We stepped to the microphone that night and sang for the first time in eight months. God had recently inspired Carroll to write a song entitled *God's Word Cannot Fail.* It was the testimony of my walk with God over the past months and seemed so appropriate to sing that night.

### God's Word Cannot Fail

*There may be no one steadfast,*
*When this generations past;*
*But God's Word cannot fail.*
*Though the sky comes crashing down,*
*Or this old world stops spinning around,*
*Still God's Word cannot fail.*
*On the truth which cannot lie,*
*Almighty God pronounced on high,*

*Even though the earth and stars should become frail*
*If the west becomes the east;*
*Or dry land consumes the seas,*
*Still God's Word cannot fail.*
*Oh, still God's Word cannot fail.*

*Though strange kingdoms should arise,*
*And the stars fall from the skies,*
*Still God's Word cannot fail;*
*And though wars and strife appear,*
*Yet God's people must not fear,*
*Still God's Word cannot fail.*

God's presence swept through us and swept through the audience as we sang. Our souls were full of thanksgiving and an indescribable joy.

True to the prophecy given in 1994, the Lord was beginning to restore what my sickness had threatened to destroy. Carroll was once again writing new songs and gradually we began accepting invitations to minister. The miracle continued. His Word cannot fail.

# Music Ministry

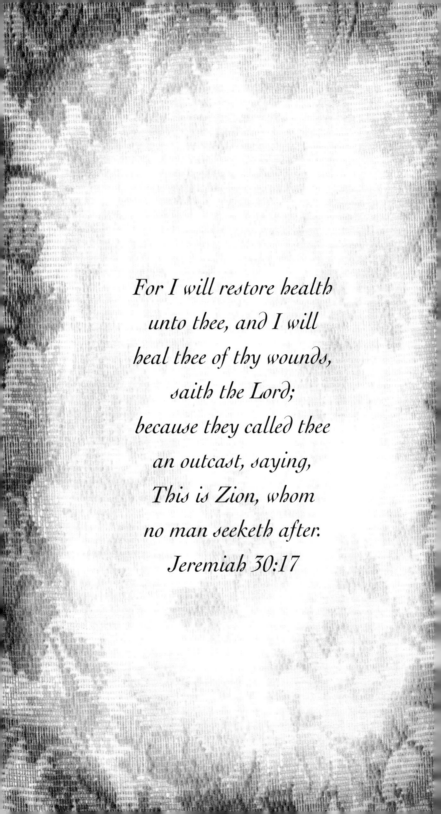

*For I will restore health*
*unto thee, and I will*
*heal thee of thy wounds,*
*saith the Lord;*
*because they called thee*
*an outcast, saying,*
*This is Zion, whom*
*no man seeketh after.*
*Jeremiah 30:17*

# Clean

Good news at last.

After my sixth treatment in August of 2000, the doctor spoke those wonderful words—cancer free! I now concentrated on getting my body back to full strength.

I returned in November for another check-up. Once again the report was good.

In January of 2001, I went to the hospital for a mammogram and an MRI. Again the report came back—cancer free.

I still return to the doctor every six months for check-ups. Two and a half years later, the report is the same. My body is totally cleansed of cancer.

I thank God for every doctor and every nurse who aided me in my total recovery. I believe they were instruments in the hands of the Lord. May God bless them for their dedication and their diligent work in this very difficult field of medicine.

One of the medical staff said to me, "Mrs. McGruder, every time you look at your body in the mirror, you are going to be depressed."

"No, I don't think so," I replied. "Every time I look in the mirror, I will praise my God for the gift of life!"

MCGRUDER, PRISCILLA E

040422

CONSULTATION REPORT

DATE: 08/16/2000

**PATIENT IDENTIFICATION:** Mrs. McGruder is a 51 year old white female with EL positive, high risk stage to cancer of the right breast, status post modified radical mastectomy on 1/31/2000. Status post chemotherapy with Adriamycin, Cytoxan and Taxotere completed 8/3/2000.

Mrs. McGruder was seen originally in February of 2000. She was noticed to have a high risk breast cancer with six positive lymph nodes. She was then started on intense chemotherapy with Adriamycin, Cytoxan followed by Taxotere. Her last chemotherapy, which was singly Taxotere, was given on 8/3/2000. This chemotherapy was poorly tolerated. There was nausea, however, almost no vomiting. In general, she was fatigued and barely recuperating.

Otherwise, this patient appears well and healthy today. She is afebrile, there are no signs of infection. She is alert, feels reasonably stable. There is increasing weakness and increasing >....................<, however, >...................< >...................< from her cancer.

Today, Mrs. Priscilla has completely recuperated from all side effects. There was a lengthy discussion as how to proceed from here. She will need follow up exams with Dr. Kakaiya every three months for two years, then she should be seen every six months, however, there is a need for yearly chest x-rays and mammograms. Bone scans will not be performed any more.

Today, this patient is alert, well. There are no abnormal findings on physical examination.

**PLAN:** This patient has received a prescription for Tamoxifen 20 mg po q AM. Osteoporosis was also discussed in detail, Os-Cal with Vitamin D should be a good supplement.

Mrs. McGruder will be referred back to Dr. Kakaiya. We will be available if there is any need for our services.


Dictated by_____
T:  08/17/2000                Juergen H. Bertram, M.D.
D:  08/16/2000
JB/cac

cc: Dr. Kakaiya


**TWIN RIVERS REGIONAL MEDICAL CENTER**                **Page 1**
**Kennett, Missouri**                                   copy

*104*

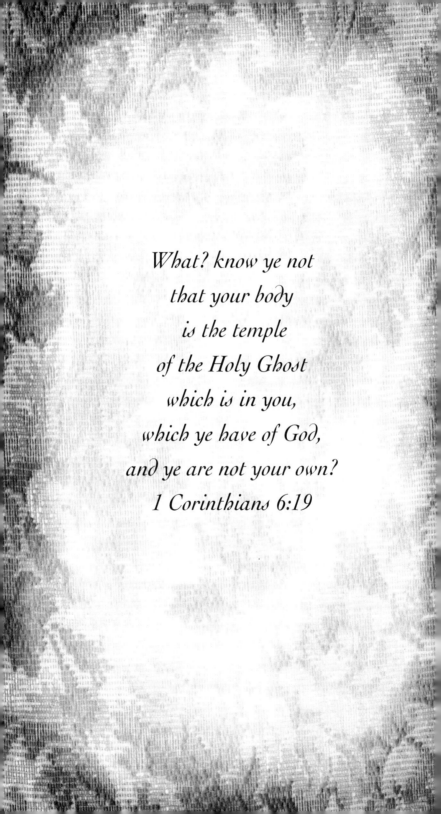

*What? know ye not*
*that your body*
*is the temple*
*of the Holy Ghost*
*which is in you,*
*which ye have of God,*
*and ye are not your own?*
*1 Corinthians 6:19*

# The Temple

Still practicing self-discipline.

Several years ago, the Lord began to talk with me about taking better care of my body. His Words came to me strongly.

> *What? know ye not that your body is the temple of the Holy Ghost which is in you, which ye have of God, and ye are not your own?*
> *1 Corinthians 6:19*

A temple needs to be cared for in the finest style possible. And so I decided to add some new disciplines to my life. I believe that healthy living has its own intrinsic rewards.

- I resolved to walk at least two miles every day.
- I quit eating a lot of fast food products.
- I go to bed early and wake up early for my time with God and my exercise.
- I quit eating after church services and concerts. I don't eat before I go to bed.
- I drink a lot of water.

I continued all these disciplines during my eight months of surgeries and chemotherapy. Then I added to these disciplines the exercises that the doctor recommended to restore the strength on the right side of my body. Eventually I was able to raise my right arm above my head.

I still continue to treat my body with great respect. God created it and He dwells in it, and so I want my temple to be the finest it can be. After all, it is the House of God.

*My daily walk.*

*What do ye imagine*
*against the Lord?*
*He will make an utter end:*
*affliction shall not rise up*
*the second time.*
*Nahum 1:9*

# No Fear

Months later...

My chemotherapy treatments were in the past and Carroll and I were singing in the state of Georgia. A disc jockey approached me and said, "Now you know that cancer could come back on the other side of your body, Priscilla."

"I do not receive that," I said to myself. "In Jesus name I will not receive that."

In the month of May 2001, I awoke at 4:00 a.m. and headed for my prayer room. As I walked down the hall-way, suddenly a terrible pain struck me on the left side of my chest. The pain was so severe that I bent over at the waist.

The words of the deejay immediately came to my mind. Something whispered to me, "Your cancer has come back. You've traveled all over telling people that

God has healed you. Now the cancer has returned. What are you going to do now?"

I went into my prayer room and reached for the Bible. A Scripture came to me that I had heard some time ago—Nahum 1:9. I opened my Bible and found the verse.

> *What do ye imagine against the Lord? He will make an utter end: affliction shall not rise up the second time.*

As I read the verse, I began shouting and praising the Lord. God had given me the reassurance I needed.

Satan will continually try to bind us with a spirit of fear. When fear comes, I take the Bible and speak it again and again. The most powerful weapon we have against the enemy is Scripture. We have the power to overcome pain and fear. We must fight with the weapon of the Word.

That day the pain left my body. It has not returned since.

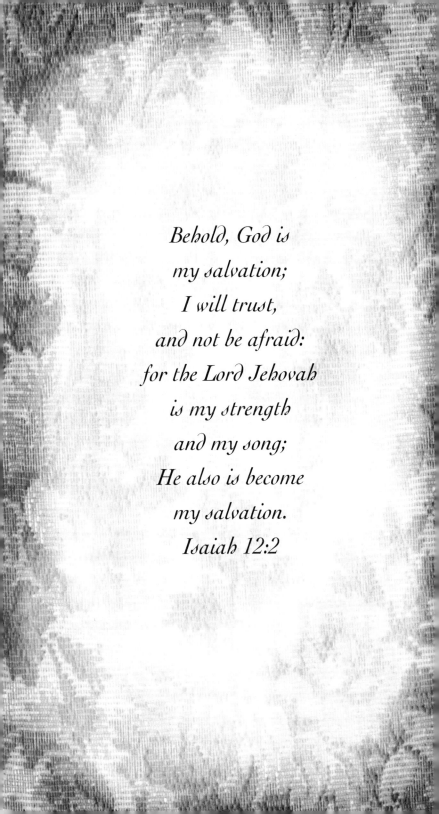

*Behold, God is
my salvation;
I will trust,
and not be afraid:
for the Lord Jehovah
is my strength
and my song;
He also is become
my salvation.*

*Isaiah 12:2*

# Thrice Born

It occurs to me that I have experienced three amazing births in my lifetime.

### 1st Birth

I made my entrance into this world on October 25, 1948. I was born on an old blue couch in our home at 320 El Paso Street, South Modesto, California. Mama and Daddy and a mid-wife were there to witness my arrival into the world. They named me Priscilla Elaine McDonald.

### 2nd Birth

When I was only six years old, I was born into the family of God. I repented of my sins and was baptized in the name of Jesus. The night He filled me with the Spirit, I was lying on the floor speaking in a heavenly language. Again, Mom and Dad were there to witness my second birth. One was kneeling on each side of me.

That same night, my Grandpa Mac was in the audience watching everything that was happening. When he witnessed the Lord filling me with His Spirit, he said, "Lord, what you're doing for my granddaughter, you can do for me."

He knelt and repented of his sins and that same night, God filled him with His Spirit. We have always called ourselves "spiritual twins." He was sixty and I was six. Definitely a night to remember.

### 3rd Birth

My journey with breast cancer has given me another new birth experience. Through times of desperation, I have found a deeper spiritual perspective than I ever had before. I have known the love of family, church members, and friends more than I realized in time of health and prosperity.

A true compassion has been born in me. Since I previously had hardly been sick a day in my life, it was impossible to empathize with the weak and frail. Now I can truly say, "I feel their pain."

In the past, Carroll and I have experienced financial blessings and the joy of ministering to great crowds of people. My sickness took all of that from us for a span of time.

In one way, we may seem to have nothing, yet we feel we have everything. The real things of life can't be measured with a number. They are too rich to be counted on a calculator. We are, of all people, most richly blessed.

And so, I have chosen for the title of this book, the name of one of Carroll's most beloved songs—*I've Just Started Living*. The Cathedrals recorded this song and made it the title song of an album they produced. In 1990 that song won the Dove Award in Nashville.

### I've Just Started Living

*I've just started living,*
*I've found me a brand new life.*
*It changed my direction,*
*Washed away all my strife.*
*I'm a new born believer;*
*It's a holy infilling;*
*My load is getting lighter;*
*My day is getting brighter,*
***I've just started living.***

*If I had hope only*
*In this world below,*
*I'd be covered with trouble;*
*There'd be no place to go;*
*But when I met Jesus,*
*And I started believing,*
*I got filled with His love,*
*I got cleansed by His blood,*
***I've just started living.***

*Now don't look at me funny,*
*You old prophet of doom,*
*I'm not one bit discouraged,*
*And I'm feeling no gloom;*
*Because I have God's Spirit,*
*And it's totally thrilling,*
*I've give up on doubting*
*There's no time for pouting,*
***I've just started living.***

The sole purpose of this book is to lift your faith to new levels of expectancy. Everyone who experiences a life threatening illness has a unique story to tell. But whatever the case, one thing remains consistent: God's Word can carry us through any challenge the Lord allows to come our way.

May every reader find new hope for the journey and may you have a great forever.

With love,

Priscilla